J. Severn Walker

Architectural Sketches, Ecclesiastical, Secular and Domestic

in Worcestershire and its borders, with historical and descriptive notes -

Vol. 1

J. Severn Walker

Architectural Sketches, Ecclesiastical, Secular and Domestic
in Worcestershire and its borders, with historical and descriptive notes - Vol. 1

ISBN/EAN: 9783337339814

Printed in Europe, USA, Canada, Australia, Japan

Cover: Foto ©Andreas Hilbeck / pixelio.de

More available books at **www.hansebooks.com**

Architectural Sketches,

ECCLESIASTICAL, SECULAR, AND DOMESTIC,

IN

WORCESTERSHIRE AND ITS BORDERS.

WITH

HISTORICAL AND DESCRIPTIVE NOTES.

BY

J. SEVERN WALKER.

Hon. Secretary to the Worcester Diocesan Architectural Society.

> " How all things glow with life and thought,
> Where'er our faithful fathers trod!
> The very ground with speech is fraught,
> The air is eloquent of God.
> In vain would doubt or mockery hide
> The buried echoes of the past;
> A voice of strength—a voice of pride—
> Here dwells amid the storm and blast."

VOL. I.

WORCESTER:
PRINTED FOR THE AUTHOR BY DEIGHTON & SON ; AND SOLD BY ALL BOOKSELLERS.
LONDON : J. MASTERS & CO., ALDERSGATE STREET & NEW BOND STREET.

THE RIGHT HONO█████████ LYTTELTON,

LORD █████

PRESIDENT OF THE WORCEST██ ████████ ███TY, ETC., ETC.,

THIS VOLUME IS, █████ ██████ DICATED,

BY HIS LORDSHIP'S ███ ██████ ██D SERVANT,

██████ SEVERN WALKER.

PREFACE TO FIRST PART.

The objects and scope of the present Work were so fully set forth in the original prospectus, that I have thought it desirable to reprint the following extract by way of introduction to the first part :—

"The architecture of this district is but little known in comparison with that of many others. The numerous publications treating of church architecture, which have been written during the last twenty years, seldom refer to Worcestershire examples ; whilst its secular and domestic remains are but cursorily noticed in works treating of that branch of art.

"A complete and comprehensive *Illustrated County History*, which has long been desired, could only be satisfactorily carried out at a great expenditure both of time and money, even if a gentleman could be found, who, possessing the requisite varied information necessary for the editorship, would be willing to undertake so important and arduous a work.

"Attempts have been made to publish detailed accounts of the churches of the counties of Northampton, York, Cambridge, and Warwick ; but in each case the project was abandoned after a volume or two had been issued, the comparatively limited circulation which publications chiefly of local interest necessarily command being insufficient to defray the great expense incurred by the costly character of the illustrations—steel plates, wood-cuts, and lithographs—with which they were enriched.

"By adopting the *Anastatic* process (whereby the artists' sketches can be multiplied to any extent, without the intervention of the engraver or lithographer), the cost of the proposed ARCHITECTURAL SKETCHES will be materially reduced ; and though not aspiring to the dignity of the elaborate works above-mentioned, or laying claim to high *artistic* excellence, it is hoped that the illustrations will be such as to convey correct impressions of the originals ; that important feature in architectural prints—faithfulness—being scrupulously maintained. Our ancient and time-honoured Churches, being the most numerous, will of course form the chief objects for illustration, due attention being at the same time being to old Manor and Court-houses, ancient Tithe Barns, Bridges, and the picturesque Half-timbered Structures which are often to be met with in out-of-the-way nooks and corners, as well as in the streets of our towns.

"Another feature of interest will be afforded by the publication of *facsimiles* of scarce old Prints and Drawings, representing buildings now destroyed or modernized.

"But whilst illustrating the architectural *antiquities* of the district, it will also be the aim of the Author to show the present state of architectural progress, by giving views of new and restored churches, parsonages, schools, and other buildings—not omitting labourers' cottages, which at the present time are deservedly occupying so much attention."

In issuing the first number of the *Architectural Sketches*, I must crave the indulgence of my Subscribers for the imperfections which I am well aware it exhibits—such as a want of clearness in some of the drawings, which have not transferred so well as I could have wished. I trust, however, that artistically faulty as the illustrations may be, they will yet be found to be faithful representations of the objects delineated ; and that the experience gained in executing these drawings will enable me to obviate their chief defects in future parts.

In the present part I have not confined myself to one particular district, or to one class of subjects, but have rather sought to interest the various subscribers by selecting from different localities the several architectural objects which it is the purpose of this publication to illustrate.

In the following pages will be found views of churches—new, restored, and unrestored ; ancient houses still remaining, and one long since demolished ; an interesting example of a mediæval bridge, &c. With one or two exceptions, no illustrations of any of these structures have ever before been published ; and some of them, as *Woodmanton*, are, I believe, quite unknown beyond their immediate localities. Future parts will contain subjects of greater architectural value than the present ; and I shall feel particularly obliged by the loan of drawings and engravings of *buildings that have been destroyed or modernized*—such representations being particularly interesting and valuable.

The historical notes which accompany the drawings are gleaned principally from Nash's "Collections," and other authorities ; but I am alone responsible for the architectural descriptions and remarks.

While deferring to the completion of the volume any detailed expression of thanks for the assistance which I have received from many quarters, I cannot let this opportunity pass without acknowledging the very kind interest manifested in the undertaking by Sir T. E. Winnington, Bart., to whom I am indebted for some valuable suggestions, as well as for the names of many subscribers. My thanks are also due to the Rev. N. G. Batt, and Mr. Dudley Male, architect, of London, for several artistic anastatic drawings ; and to Mr. Noake for his experienced aid in revising the proof sheets as they passed through the press.

J. S. W.

Sansome Lodge, Worcester,
Lent, 1862.

A TABLE OF THE NAMES AND DATES OF THE DIFFERENT STYLES OF

ENGLISH MEDIÆVAL ARCHITECTURE.

STYLE.	KINGS.	DATE.
NORMAN, OR ENGLISH ROMANESQUE.	William I.	1066
	William II.	1087
	Henry I.	1100
	Stephen	1135
	Henry II.	1154 to 1189
FIRST-POINTED, OR EARLY ENGLISH.	Richard I.	1189
	John	1199
	Henry III.	1327 to 1377
MIDDLE-POINTED, OR DECORATED ENGLISH.	Edward I.	1272
	Edward II.	1307
	Edward III.	1327 to 1377
THIRD-POINTED, OR PERPENDICULAR ENGLISH.	Richard II.	1377
	Henry IV.	1399
	Henry V.	1413
	Henry VI.	1422
	Edward IV.	1461
	Edward V.	1483
	Richard III.	1483
	Henry VII.	1485
	Henry VIII.	1509 to 1546

LIST OF SUBSCRIBERS.

Addenbrooke, Rev. E., Smethwick
Aldham, Rev. Harcourt, Stoke Prior Vicarage
Allsopp, Henry, Esq., Hindlip House, Worcester (Proof)
Amphlett, Rev. Martin, Church Lench Rectory
Amphlett, Rev. Joseph, Hampton Lovett Rectory
Appleton, J. Reed, Esq., F.S.A., Western Hill, Durham
Arthure, Rev. B., All Saints' Rectory, Worcester
Boughton, Sir Charles, Bart., Downton Hall, Ludlow (Proof)
Baker, Slade, Esq., Sandbourne, Bewdley
Baker, Rev. Slade, Clifton-upon-Teme Vicarage
Baker, Miss, Perth Cottage, Ryde, Isle of Wight (Proof)
Barber, Rev. F. H., Sedgeberrow Rectory
Barneby, J. H., Esq., Saltmarsh Castle, Bromyard (Proof)
Barnett, R., Esq., Cumberland House, Worcester
Bate, Charles J., Esq., Darnard's Green, Malvern
Bate, Miss, The Lady Hills, Kenilworth
Batt, Rev. N. J., Norton Vicarage, Evesham (Two copies)
Biddulph, Robert, Esq., Ledbury (Proof)
Binns, R. W., Esq., F.S.A., Worcester (Proof)
Bolton, W., Esq., 3, Highgate Rise, London
Bourne, Rev. Joseph G., Broome Rectory, Stourbridge (Proof)
Bradley, Rev. Edward, Denton Rectory, Hunts.
Brown-Westhead, J. P., Esq., M.P., Lea Castle, Kidderminster (Proof)
Brown, T. J., Esq., The Moor, Hereford, (Three Proof copies)
Bund, Miss, Bengeworth House, Evesham (Proof)
Burrow, Rev. H. H., Severn Stoke
Burrow, Mr. W. B., Eastnor Villa, The Link, Malvern
Burrow, Mr. J. S., Great Malvern
Carden, H. D., Esq. (Proof)
Cattley, Rev. R., Minor Canon of Worcester Cathedral
Chalk, T., Esq., Worcester (Proof)
Chamberlain, J. H., Esq., Professor of Architecture, Queen's College, Birmingham (Proof)
Clarke, Rev. H., Northfield Rectory (Proof)
Clarke, G. Row, Esq., Architect, London (Proof)
Claughton, Rev. T. L., Hon. Canon of Worcester, Kidderminster (Proof)
Claughton, The Hon. Mrs. (Proof)
Cocks, Reginald, Esq., Charing Cross, London (Proof)
Collis, Rev. J. D., D.D., Hon. Canon of Worcester, Grammar School, Bromsgrove
Colvile, Lieut.-General, Kempsey House, Worcester
Cookes, Rev. H. Winford, Astley Rectory
Corbett, G., Esq., Foregate Street, Worcester
Coucher, Martin S., Esq., M.D., Weymouth (Proof)
Coxwell, C. R., Esq., South Bank, Malvern (Proof)
Dudley, The Right Hon. the Earl of, Witley Court (Proof)
Dryden, Sir H. E. L., Bart., Canons Ashby, Northamptonshire
Davis, E., Esq., Northwick, Worcester (Proof)
Davis, T. H., Esq., Orleton, Stamford
Day, H., Esq., Architect, Worcester
Deighton, Miss, Worcester
Dickins, Rev. C., Tardebigge Vicarage
Dolman, F. T., Esq., Architect, London
Domvile, Wm., Esq., Thornhill, Bray, Ireland
Douglas, Rev. The Hon. H., Hanbury Rectory (Proof)
Douglas, Rev. A. J., Mathon Vicarage
Douglas, Rev. W. W., Rural Dean, Salwarpe Rectory
Dowdeswell, W., Esq., Pull Court, Tewkesbury (Two copies)
Dunhill, James, Esq., Doncaster (Proof)
Dunhill, Wm., Esq., Doncaster
Dyson, Miss, The Pleasance, Great Malvern (Proof)
Easterfield, E., Esq., Doncaster
Edwards, the late C. J., Esq., Broadward, Leominster
Egan, Miss, Ivy Bank, Worcester
Elkington, Fredk., Esq., Selly Wood, Northfield
Elmslie, E. W., Esq., Architect, Malvern
Essington, W. E., Esq., Ribbesford House (Proof)
Fletcher, Thomas Wm., Esq., M.A., F.R.S., F.S.A., Lawneswood House, Stourbridge (Proof)
Foley, The Right Hon. Lord (Proof)
Foley, H. W., Esq., M.P., Prestwood (Proof)
Forester, Rev. R. T., Elmley Lodge, Brandon Parade, Leamington (Proof)
Foster, W. O., Esq., M.P., Stourton Castle (Proof)
Fowler, Rev. R. Rodney, Minor Canon of Worcester Cathedral
Freer, The Venerable R. L., D.D., Archdeacon of Hereford, Bishopston Rectory (Proof)

Glynne, Sir Stephen, Bart., Hawarden Castle, Chester
Goldingham, H. G., Esq., Worcester
Gresley, R. A. Douglas, Esq., High Park, Droitwich (Proof)
Gresley, Major, Winterdyne, Bewdley (Proof)
Grier, Rev. J. W., Amblecote Parsonage, Stourbridge
Grosvenor, Wm., Esq., Kidderminster (Proof)
Guest, E. R., Esq., Thorney Cottage, Dodnham
Harvey, Mr. Charles, Kidderminster (Two copies)
Hartshorne, Mrs., Rose Hill, Worcester
Hastings, Rev. H. J., Rural Dean, Hon. Canon of Worcester, Martley Rectory (Proof)
Havergal, Rev. W. H., Hon. Canon of Worcester, Shareshill (Proof)
Havergal, Rev. F.T., Minor Canon of Hereford Cathedral, Rector of Pipe and Lyde
Haywood, E., Esq., Bayton Villa, Clifton-upon-Teme (Proof)
Haywood, Mr. J. S., Broad Street, Worcester
Hill, Canning, Esq., Solicitor, Worcester
Hill, Rev. H. T., Rural Dean, Fekenham Rectory, Bromyard (Proof)
Hill, Rev. Melsup, Shelsley Beauchamp Rectory
Hill, R., Esq., Orleton Court, Herefordshire
Hill, T. Rowley, Esq., Catherine Hill House, Worcester (Proof)
Hodgkinson, Mr. W., Kidderminster, (Three Proof copies)
Holden, Hyla, Esq., Worcester
Holland, Rev. T. E. M., Stoke Bliss Rectory
Holloway, Mrs. B., Hopton, Bromyard
Holmes, E. Esq., Architect, Birmingham
Hooke, Thomas, Esq., Norton Hall, Worcester (Proof)
Hopkins, W. J., Esq., Architect to Worcester Church Extension Society, &c. (Proof)
Hopton, Rev. W. P., Froome Bishop Rectory, Bromyard
Hughes, W. S. P., Esq., Langhern House, Martley (Proof)
James, Rev. J. C., Saint John's, Worcester
Johnstone, Lieut.-Col., Tything, Worcester (Proof)
Knight, E. Winn, Esq., M.P.
Knott, W. Esq., Lower Wick, Worcester.
Lyttelton, The Right Hon. Lord, Hagley Hall (Proof)
Lyttelton, Rev. The Hon. W. H., Hon. Canon of Worcester, Hagley Rectory (Proof)
Lygon, The Hon. Frederick, M.P., F.S.A., All Souls' College, Oxford (Proof)
Lechmere, Sir E. A. H., Bart., Rhydd Court (Proof)
Lambert, Rev. Brooke, Saint John's, Worcester
Lander, Rev. C., Limbrigg Vicarage
Laslett, Wm., Esq., Abberton Hall
Lea, Rev. J. T., Far Forest Parsonage, Bewdley
Lea, Rev. Wm., Hon. Canon of Worcester, St. Peter's Vicarage, Droitwich
Lea, J. Wheeley, Esq., Stanfield House, Worcester (Proof)
Lea, J. Wildman, Esq., Netherton, Bewdley
Lees, Edwin, Esq., F.L.S., Green Hill Summit, Worcester
Lincoln Diocesan Architectural Society
Loscombe, The Misses, College Green, Worcester (Proof)
Mackay, Mr. J., 38, Tything, Worcester
Mackarness, Rev. G. R., Ilam Vicarage, Ashbourne
Male, Dudley, Esq., Architect, London
Markland, J. H., Esq., D.C.L. F.S.A., Lansdown Crescent, Bath
Marriott, Rev. F. A., Chaddesley Corbett Vicarage
Marshall, Mrs., College Yard, Worcester (Proof)
Mence, W., Esq., 7, Clayton Square, Liverpool
Miller, Rev. J. J., Bockleton Rectory, Tenbury (Proof)
Morris, P. S., Esq., Woodmanton, Clifton-upon-Teme
Mottram, Rev. J. C. M., Kidderminster
Moore, John, Esq., Home Castle, Clifton-upon-Teme
Munn, Rev. G. S., Madresfield Rectory
Murray, Rev. G. W., Bromsgrove Vicarage (Proof)
Northwick, The Right Hon. Lord, Northwick Park. (Proof)
Newcomb, Rev. E. J., Leigh, Worcester
Newman, T. Esq., High House, Upper Sapey
Nicholson, T., Esq., Diocesan Architect, Hereford
Norton, John, Esq., Architect, London
Onley, J. D., Esq., Dransford, Worcester
Onslow, Rev. Phipps, Upper Sapey Rectory
Osborne, Mrs., Britannia Square, Worcester
Pakington, The Right Hon. Sir J. S., Bart., G.C.B., M.P., Westwood Park. (Two copies)
Pakington, J. Slaney, Esq., Kent's Green, Worcester (Two copies)
Parker, Rev. W., Little Cumberton Rectory (Proof)
Parker, Mrs. John, Wood-isle, Worcester (Proof)

Parker, J. H., Esq., Oxford
Pateshall, Mrs. Burnam, Allensmore Court, Hereford
Pattrick, C. G. H. St., Esq., 2, Worcester Terrace, Clifton, Bristol (Proof)
Pepys, Rev. H. G., Hallow Vicarage (Proof)
Perceval, Rev. H., Elmley Lovett Rectory
Perrins, Mr. J. D., Worcester
Philpott, Rev. T. Belloroughton (Proof)
Phipps, Mrs. H. Barré, Llwyn-dû, Abergavenny (Proof)
Pilcher, Miss, Draycot Lodge, Kempsey (Proof)
Plantre, Rev. R. W., Corfe-Mullen, Dorsetshire
Pocock, J. Innes, Esq., Puckrup Hall, Tewkesbury (Proof)
Porter, Miss, Birlingham (Proof)
Preedy, F., Esq., Architect, London
Price, W., Esq., Benhall, Ross
Prichard, Rev. R., Rural Dean, Newbold-upon-Stour Rectory
Pritchard, John, Esq., M.P., Broseley
Rushout, The Hon. Miss, Burford House, Tenbury (Proof)
Raymond, Rev. W. F., Rural Dean, Stockton Rectory
Ricardo, Osman, Esq., M.P., Bromesberrow
Roberts, G. E., Esq., Geological Society of London, Somerset House
Rowe, H., Esq., Architect, Worcester
Rufford, Mrs., Great Alne, Warwickshire
Rufford, Rev. W., Sapey Pitchard Rectory
Russell, J. Watts, Esq., Ilam Hall Ashburne (Proof)
Shrewsbury and Talbot, The Right Hon. the Earl of (Proof)
Sitwell, Evelyn P., Esq., M.P., F.S.A., Lower Eatington Park, (Proof)
Sale, Rev. C. J., Holt Rectory (Proof)
Sandars, Mrs., Parkfield, Derby
Sanders, Rev. R., Minor Canon of Worcester Cathedral, Cropthorne Vicarage
Seymour, Rev. R., Rural Dean, Hon. Canon of Worcester, Kinwarton Rectory
St. Aubyn, J. P., Esq., Architect, London
Shipway, J., Esq., Architect, Malvern
Shuker, Rev. H., Wichenford Vicarage
Simpson, Rev. J. D., Montpellier Mansion, Cheltenham

Skidmore, F. A., Esq., Coventry (Proof)
Skinner, Rev. James, Newland, Malvern
Smith, Rev. I. Gregory, Tedstone Delamere Rectory
Smith, Rev. T. Ayscough, Tenbury Vicarage
Smith, Mrs., Shelsley Walsh
Smith, Robert, Esq., Crowle, Worcester
Stallard, Josiah, Esq., Worcester
Stock, T. S., Esq., Northfield
Stone, E. G., Esq., Cumber's Court
Stuart, J. E., Esq., 172, New Bond Street, London (Proof)
Sylvester, G. J., Esq., Tything, Worcester
Taylor, Miss, Wollaston, Wellingborough
Thomas, The Misses, Boughton Fields, Worcester
Thorn, Rev. Wm., Thames House, Worcester (Proof)
Thorp, The Venerable T., B.D., Archdeacon of Bristol, Kemerton Rectory (Proof)
Truefitt, George, Esq., Architect, London
Venables, T. A., Esq., Britannia Lodge, Worcester
Vernon, Harry Foley, Esq., M.P., Hanbury Hall (Proof)
Worcester, The Right Rev. the Lord Bishop of (Proof)
Winnington, Sir T. E., Bart., M.P., Stanford Court (Proof)
Winnington, Lady
Winnington, Major, The Shrubbery, Stanford (Proof)
Winnington, Miss (Proof)
Walker, G. J. A., Esq., Norton Villa, Worcester (Proof)
Walker, J. Smith, Esq., Knightwick (Proof)
Walters, Miss, Condover, Shrewsbury
Warner, Rev. C., Wribbenhall, Bewdley
Watts, W. T., Esq., Cafton Hackett (Proof)
Whatman, James, Esq., Vinters, Maidstone, Kent
Whitfield, Rev. G. T., Puddlestone Rectory, Leominster (Proof)
Wicksted, Mrs., Shakenhurst
Willis, J. W., Bund, Esq., Upper Wick House, Worcester
Wood, Rev. J. R., Canon of Worcester Cathedral (Proof)
Wood, Joseph, Esq., Lansdown Villa, Worcester (Proof)
Wood, Mr. John, Foregate Street, Worcester
Woolrych, Rev. W. H., Crowle Vicarage, Worcester (Proof)
Wright, Rev. J. H. C., Wolferlow Vicarage, Tenbury

S. John the Baptist's Church, Bagley.
Previously to its Restoration.

Hagley.

AT the time of Domesday survey, William Fitz Ansculph was lord paramount of Hagley, which was held under him by one Roger, who assumed the surname of *Haggaley* from the place of his residence, as was common in those times. The descendants of Roger continued here till the 23rd of Edward III., when Edmund de Haggaley disposed of both the manor and advowson for 100 marks of silver to Sir John Boutetort, lord paramount in right of his wife Joan, sister of Roger de Somery, whose family succeeded the Paganels and Fitz Ansculph in the barony of Dudley and lordship of Hagley. Though the manor was purchased by Sir John Boutetort, Henry de Haggaley, heir to Edmund, recovered it the 47th of Edward III., together with the advowson and six acres of land in Clent, called Cowbach, (where the body of the murdered St. Kenelm was discovered). Henry de Haggaley sold it in 1411 to Thomas Walwyn, who disposed of it to Lady Bergavenny, and she left it to her grandson, Sir James Boteler, son of the Earl of Ormond, and afterwards Earl of Wiltshire. Being executed at Newcastle for his adherence to the house of Lancaster, all his lands were confiscated to the crown; and Hagley was granted by Edward IV. successively to Fulk Stafford, Thomas Prout, his consort Elizabeth Woodville, and the Abbey of Westminster. Thomas Butler, younger brother of the Earl of Wiltshire, getting into the King's favour, procured the restoration of the latter's lands and manors, including Hagley, which descended to Sir John St. Leger, who in 1564 sold it to Sir John Lyttelton, of Frankley, Knight.

It would be going beyond the scope of this work to give a detailed history of the ancient and distinguished family of Lyttelton; but a name so intimately connected with the history of the county cannot be passed over without a few brief historical remarks.

The Lytteltons came originally from Littleton, in the Vale of Evesham, where they were settled early in the twelfth century, and whence they took their name. They inherited Frankley by marriage in the time of Henry III. Thomas Litelton, Sheriff of Worcestershire in the reign of Henry V., had a daughter who married Thomas Westcote of Westcote, county of Devon, Esq. Their son Thomas Lyttelton was the noted Judge and author of the Tenures; he died in 1481, and was buried in Worcester Cathedral. From him descended the Lytteltons of Frankley, Spetchley, and Pillaton. Thomas of Spetchley was ancestor of Edward Lyttelton, Keeper of the Great Seal in the reign of Charles I.; and of Sir Thomas Lyttelton, Speaker of the House of Commons. Some of the Frankley branch of the family were connected with the gunpowder plot conspirators. Holbeach House, where they made their last stand, was the residence of Stephen Lyttelton, who, together with Robert Winter, was concealed for some time at Hagley, being ultimately betrayed by one of the servants. Thomas, son of John Lyttelton, and Muriel, or Maryell, daughter of Lord

Chancellor Bromley, was created a baron in 1618. He was a zealous supporter of the Royal cause during the civil wars, and his house at Frankley was burnt to prevent it from falling into the hands of the Parliamentary forces. His great-grandson George Lyttelton, the statesman and the man of letters, to whose friendship with Pope, Thomson, Shenstone, and most of the celebrated authors of his day, the classic associations connected with Hagley are due, was created Baron Lyttelton of Frankley in 1757. His brother William Henry, having been governor of Jamaica and ambassador to Portugal, was raised to the dignity of Baron Westcote of Ballamore, in the peerage of Ireland, in the year 1776. By the death of the second Lord Lyttelton, without issue, A.D. 1779, the title became extinct; but was revived in the person of his uncle, Lord Westcote, in 1794, from whom the present noble Lord is directly descended.

The Church is situated within the Park, near the Hall, and is dedicated to St. John the Baptist.

Before the recent restoration and enlargement, it consisted of chancel, nave, north and south aisles, and south porch, with a wooden bell-turret at the west end of the nave. The body of the church was chiefly of the Middle-pointed style, the arcades consisting of plain pointed arches resting on octagonal piers. The chancel was re-built by the first Lord Lyttelton, in 1754. Contrary to what might have been expected of a period in which an "elegant classic building" was commonly thought to be most suitable for a house of prayer, the new chancel was erected in imitation of our old national Pointed styles of architecture. This was, doubtless, owing to the antiquarian tastes of Dr. C. Lyttelton, Dean of Exeter, president of the Society of Antiquaries, and afterwards Bishop of Carlisle, at whose cost the ceiling and cornice of the new building were adorned with shields bearing, in their proper colours, the arms of the family from the time of Henry III. The nave and aisles were provided with new windows, pews, and gallery, at the same time.

A few years ago a public subscription was raised throughout the county in order to present Lord Lyttelton with a Testimonial expressive of the general appreciation of the manner in which he exercised the duties of his high office of Lord Lieutenant; and also to mark the high sense entertained of his Lordship's zealous exertions in promoting every good work, especially those connected with education and the church. The enlargement and thorough restoration of Hagley Church having long been desired by Lord Lyttelton, it was determined that the money thus contributed should be expended in carrying out that good work, which would form a more useful and lasting Testimonial, and one far more in accordance with his Lordship's wishes than the tasteless and unmeaning pieces of plate which public marks of esteem so frequently consist in.[*]

Mr. Street was employed to design the new works, which were completed, and the church re-opened in April, 1858.

The old structure was entirely re-built, with the exception of the nave arcades, the east

---

[*] These remarks do not, of course, apply to really artistic works of art, such as the Testimonial presented by this county to another of its public benefactors not long since.

end of the south aisle, and the north wall ; the ground plan being extended by the addition of a vestry and organ chamber on the north side of the chancel, and by lengthening the nave and aisles one way westward. The chancel floor is raised four steps above the level of the nave, and paved with encaustic tiles. At the south side of the sanctuary are three elegant sedilia, and on the opposite side is a recessed credence, while the wall beneath the lofty sill of the east window is provided with rich hangings. The wide and lofty chancel arch is supported on polished marble shafts with carved capitals. The stone pulpit is likewise enriched with marble shafts and panels. The lectern, stalls, and subsellæ are of oak ; the westernmost stalls on either side being used as prayer desks, and having peculiar *spiky* poppy heads. The chancel is lighted by the east window and two windows on the south side only, the space round the altar being in comparative obscurity, by which the appearance of the painted east window is enhanced, but which would materially interfere with the effect of a reredos, should one ever be erected. Indeed, there is rather a deficiency of light throughout the church ; though the proposed tower, with its west window, would, if carried out, tend to obviate this objection. The roofs are open, well designed, and of deal. The open seats in the nave are also of deal, with carved traceried ends. It is surely a mistake to expend in carving *deal* money that would go a good way towards providing *plain oak standards*. The painted windows at the east end of the chancel and the west end of the south aisle, as well as the porch, are memorials of the late lamented Lady Lyttelton. The east window of the south aisle is to the memory of the wife of W. Robins, Esq., and the west window in the north aisle to the late rector, the Rev. J. Turner, who died in 1847. The mural marble tablets to the Lyttletons have been divested of urns and other incongruous ornaments, and placed at the west end, where the inscriptions can easily be read, while at the same time they are unobtrusive. In the north wall is a moulded and crocketed recessed arch containing a plain tomb, on the top of which is a bold and richly foliated cross of early First-pointed character, the stem issuing out of the mouth of a lizard, or some kind of fabulous reptile. The piers and arches between the nave and aisles are not by any means graceful or well proportioned, and, except for their antiquity and associations, were hardly worth preserving in so extensive a rebuilding. On the eastern gable of the nave is a stone bell-cot for one bell, surmounted by a metal cross ; but the general character of the exterior will be best learnt by referring to the view of the church given as a frontispiece to this volume.

It were much to be wished that so satisfactory a restoration could be completed by the erection of the tower and spire, which is much needed to give dignity to the exterior of the sacred structure, and to " point out from far the holy seat of worship," it being now quite invisible at any distance.

Hagley became the principal residence of the Lytteltons of Frankley after their house at that place was destroyed. The present mansion was erected by the first Lord, from the designs of Sanderson Miller, of Radway, Warwickshire. It is a plain uniform stone structure, in the cold classic style in vogue throughout the last century ; and stands in the open park, entirely unconnected with gardens, out-houses, or any of the usual appurtenances of a dwelling-house, which gives it more the appearance of a public edifice than a private residence. There are, however, some fine rooms in the interior, stored with valuable books, paintings, and other works of art. In one of the rooms is an old carved oak chimney-piece, the only relic of the old house, which stood not far from the present one.

Hagley contains an unusual number of private houses, many of them of large size, but all, without exception, are destitute of the slightest architectural merit. A brick cottage now building, from the designs of Mr. J. H. Chamberlain, near to the rectory, promises, however, to be a really artistic structure.

A family of the name of Penn flourished at Harborough, in this parish, for four centuries. The old half-timbered house in which they lived still remains.

A Chapel of Ease, dedicated to St. James, has been erected in the hamlet of Blakedown, from Mr. Street's designs. It is a simple Early-pointed building, consisting of chancel and nave, with an over-hanging bell-cot at the west end.

Elmley Lovett.

IN the time of the Conqueror the manor of Elmley, or as it was then written Almeleia, belonged to Rafe Todeny or Thoney. It afterwards came into the possession of the Lovetts, who held many estates in this county, and made Elmley their chief place of residence, giving their name to this as well as to the adjoining parish of Hampton Lovett. Sir John Lovett, Knight, having no male heir, the name became extinct here, and their possessions fell to Beauchamp, Earl of Warwick, as heir to Thoney. By the attainder of the Earl of Warwick, 15 Henry VII., the manor of Elmley fell to the crown ; and was granted by Henry VIII. to Sir Robert Acton, second son of Richard Acton of Sutton in this county. At the death of his grandson, Sir John Acton, it was divided among his four daughters, one of whom married Robert Townshend, descended from a younger branch of the ancient family of Townshend of Raynham, ennobled in the reign of Charles II. by the creation of Horatio Townshend Viscount Townshend de Raynham.

Robert Townshend added to the Elmley property (he inherited with his wife) by purchase. Having been held by his family for four generations, it passed, in default of direct male heirs, into the hands of George Townshend Forester, Esq., younger brother of the first Lord Forester of Willey in the county of Salop, and has lately been purchased of his son, the Rev. R. T. Forester, by W. Orme Foster, Esq., M.P.

The Church occupies a commanding situation :—

> " Standing upon a hill, a gentle hill,
> Green, and of mild declivity,"

away from the village, and with but very few houses in its immediate vicinity. The spire

The Lodge.

Churchyard Cross.   The Church of S. Michael.

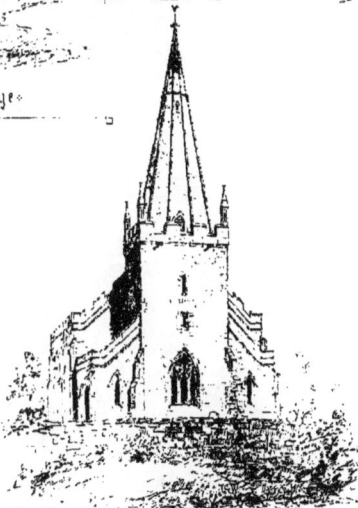

Elmley Lovett.

is visible from the railway a little to the south of the Hartlebury station. With the exception of the tower and spire the church was entirely rebuilt about 1839, in the debased sort of Gothic common at that early period of the revival of the true principles of Pointed architecture, and is as devoid of interest of any kind as such buildings usually are. It is however substantially built of squared ashlar, and has an open roof. An embattled parapet extends round the building, which is lighted by a uniform range of large lancets on each side, with a triplet at the east end of the shallow chancel. In the lower part of the tower is a good three-light Middle-pointed window, the upper portion of the tower being Third-pointed.

The base and part of the shaft of the **Churchyard Cross** remain on the south side of the church; and adjoining the eastern side of the churchyard is a small 17th-century house, with a good chimney of the period.

Philip Hawford, the last Abbot of Evesham, was rewarded for his subserviency in resigning that famous monastery to the King, with a pension of £240 a year, and the rectory of Elmley Lovett. The pension, however, was not continued after his promotion to the Deanery of Worcester.

The church is stated by Nash to be dedicated to St. Michael; it is also claimed in honour of St. Lawrence.

The living is now in the patronage of Christ's College, Cambridge; the present rector being the Rev. H. Perceval, M.A.

According to Nash, the original manor-house was situated north-west of the church, at a little distance from it.

The old mansion, known as "**The Lodge**," was erected by the Townshends; Robert, who married Elizabeth Acton, dying in 1634, whilst the date of 1635 in one of the gables probably indicates the year in which the house was completed.

It is one of the best examples of a half-timbered structure remaining in the county; the combination of gables in the principal front producing an unusually picturesque effect. The timbers in the gables are ornamentally disposed, chiefly in the form of quatrefoils : in one of these is the date, as before mentioned, and beneath the words NISI DOMINUS. The chimneys are similar to those usually found in houses of this date ; one of them on the garden side is carried up in front of and so as partially to hide two dormer windows.

With the exception of the insertion of long sash windows, —at no recent period, however,—and the loss of some of the chimney tops and gable finials, the exterior remains in pretty much its original state, though looking rather dilapidated and forlorn, a few rooms only having been inhabited for many years past.

An avenue of elms leads up to the house from the public road ; and the footway to the church passes through a small umbrageous avenue.

Hampton Lovett.

HAMPTON LOVETT once belonged to the Beauchamps; it became afterwards the property of the Lovetts, a family living at Elmley Lovett. The Lovetts becoming extinct, it passed to the Blounts, one of whom, Sir Edward Blount, was raised to the dignity of a baron, by the title of Lord Mountjoy, in the reign of Edward IV. The manor, estates, &c., afterwards passed by purchase to Sir John Pakington, Knight.

The name of Pakington occurs in the foundation of Kenilworth Priory, *temp.* Henry I.; and afterwards it is found mentioned as founding, A.D. 1322, a chantry in Chelmscote, in the lordship of Brayle, in Warwickshire, which belonged to the family. The Pakingtons first came into this county by the marriage of John Pakington with a daughter of the ancient family of Washbourne of Stanford, about the end of the reign of Henry VI. Sir John Pakington, one of their sons, was in great favour with Henry VIII., who made him a Welsh judge, and granted that during life he should wear his hat in the king's presence whenever he chose; and that he should not be compelled to take any office upon him, or suffer any penalty for refusing the same. The king also bestowed upon him the suppressed nunnery of *Westwood;* he having previously purchased the manor, &c., of Hampton. "He grew," says Habingdon, "to such an hyghthe as from his house are now descended one viscount and two baronets. The first is Sir John Scudamore of Hom Lacey, county of Hereford, visc. Sligo, heir in the 4th degree to Ursula, da. and coheir of this Sir John Pakington. The second, Sir Thomas Lytelton, of Frankley, sixth heir in the same degree to Briget, daughter and coheir of the same knight: the third, Sir John Pakington, of Hampton Lovett, bart., heir in the same degree to Robert Pakington, third brother of the great Sir John Pakington; which knight, besides lands and large portions distributed between his two daughters and coheirs, left Hampton Lovet, with other revenues, to Sir Thomas Pakington, son and heir of this Robert Pakington, and father of Sir John Pakington, who flourished once in queen Eliz. court."

The above-mentioned Robert Pakington was born at Stanford,[*] in 1537; he was member for London, and is said by Stowe to have been murdered in the streets of that city by the Papists whom he had opposed. The Sir John Pakington who lived at the time of the civil wars was a staunch supporter of the royal cause, and suffered severely for his loyalty, having to compound with the Parliament for his estates by two several payments of £5,500 and £1,300, including costs and charges. His estates in Worcestershire and Buckinghamshire were sequestered, and he was himself imprisoned in the Tower of London. His total losses for the cause of loyalty, including £200 for the "repairs of Westwood House after the

---

[*] Sir Thomas E. Winnington, Bart., has in his possession, at Stanford Court, a brass plate from old Stanford Bridge (over which they would have to pass from the former place to Hampton), bearing the following inscription, as perfect as on the day it was engraved:—
"*Pray for Haufrey Pakyndon Esquyer burat in Stanford which payd for ye workmanshepe and makyng of this bryggy the whiche was rered and made the fyrst day of may and in the fyrst yere of ye Rayne of kyng Edward ye VI.*"

+ The Church-from the S-E.

The Court-House. Destroyed in y 17ᵗʰ Cent.ᵗ
From an old Painting at Westwood Park

Hampton Lovett.

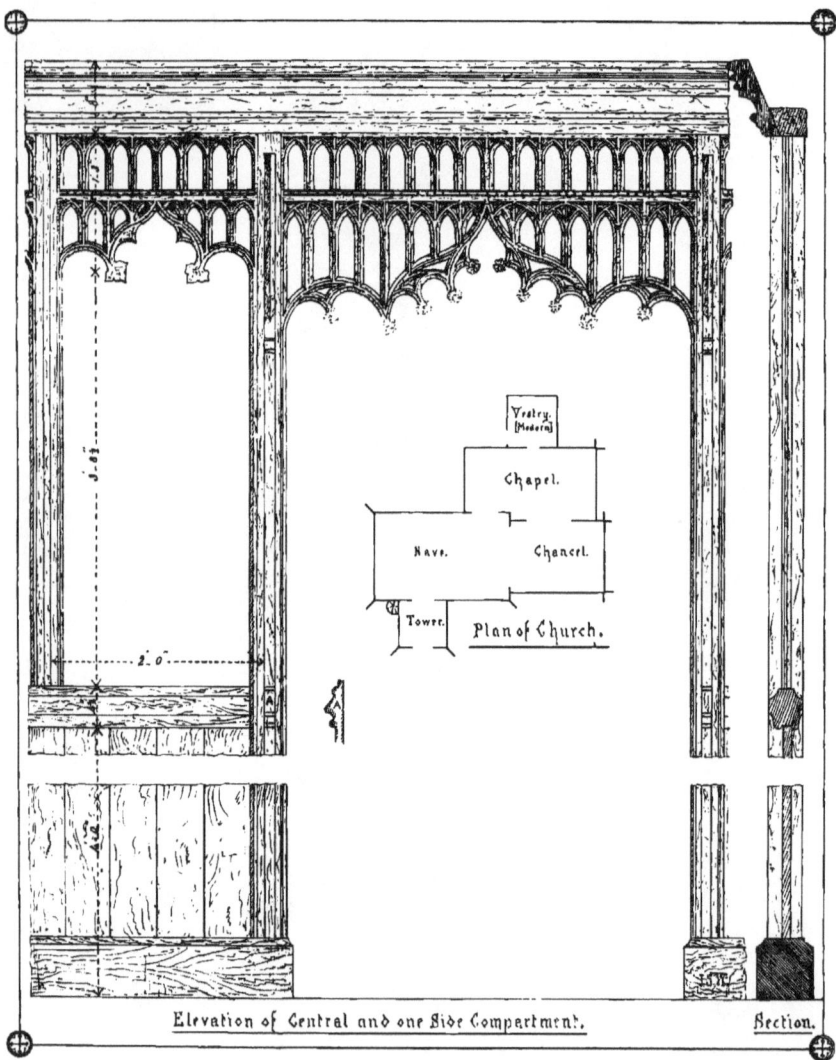

Vestry.
[Modern]

Chapel.

Nave.

Chancel.

Tower.

Plan of Church.

Elevation of Central and one Side Compartment.

Section.

Chancel Screen, formerly in S. Mary and All Saints' Church, Hampton Lovett.

Scots," amounted to £20,348. He was taken prisoner at the battle of Worcester, but soon released ; for he was so much beloved in the county that no witnesses would speak against him. He represented Worcestershire and Aylesbury in Parliament, and died in 1679, having held the title and estates for the long period of fifty-five years. His wife, Dorothy, daughter of Lord Coventry, was called "The good Lady Pakington," and is said to have written *The Whole Duty of Man*, in which she would probably be assisted by her friends Drs. Hammond and Fell. Sir John Pakington, the grandson of the above, represented Worcestershire in Parliament from the age of nineteen, excepting one Parliament, till his death, which happened in 1727, at the age of fifty-six. It is stated on his monument that he was "loyal to his king and faithful to his country ; and that he spoke without reserve, neither fearing nor flattering those in power, but despising all their offers of preferment upon base and dishonourable terms of compliance." This Sir John Pakington is supposed to have furnished the original of Addison's famous character of Sir Roger de Coverley. Subsequently to this period no member of the family appears to have taken any very prominent part in public affairs, till the present baronet commenced his useful career as a statesman, and as an able advocate of social progress.

The Church of Hampton Lovett, though possessing no very striking architectural feature, is eminently a *picturesque* structure ; this is owing, in a great measure, to the variety of outline occasioned by the somewhat unusual position of the tower, the *sanctus* bell-cot, and the large chapel attached to its north side ; the effect being further heightened by the trees with which the sacred building is nearly surrounded.

It is dedicated to S. Mary and All Saints ; and is situated about a mile and a half to the north of Droitwich, near the line of the Oxford, Worcester, and Wolverhampton railway, which passes within a few yards of the east end, and commands a good view of the church.

The ground plan comprises chancel, north chapel, vestry, nave, and south tower. Traces of Norman work occur in the walls ; the blocked-up north doorway is also in this style, the arch being supported by cylindrical shafts, with plain cushion capitals, and having the star ornament.

Middle-pointed windows, with reticulated tracery, have been inserted north, west, and south of the nave. The rest of the building is of the fifteenth century, or Third-pointed style. The east window is pointed, of three lights ; the side windows of the chancel and chapel are good examples of two and three-light square-headed windows of the period. The chancel communicates with the nave and chapel by wide four-centred arches, with continuous mouldings. The old Rood-screen was of very late date, and enriched with colour and gilding ; but it did not fit its position well, the top extending considerably above the spring of the arch ; it is, however, a matter of regret that it could not be applied to some other purpose in the church, instead of being removed altogether. The chapel is very broad, and extends the whole length of the chancel and about one third that of the nave.

Among Roger Dodsworth's MSS., in the Bodleian Library, Oxon., is the foundation deed of a chantry in S. Anne's chapel at Hampton Lovett : "two priests to celebrate mass, one

at the altar of S. John Baptist, and the other at the altar of S. Anne, for the souls of Alice
Lady Stury, Sir John Blount, and Elizabeth his wife, parents of the said Alice," who is also
said to have built the chapel. The ordination of the chantry was confirmed by Bishop
Thomas Peverell, October 18, 1414. The architecture of the chapel and the chancel agree with
the above date; but the east window of the former is, apparently, a more recent insertion,
having unfoliated four-centred lights, beneath a square head. The date, 1561, inscribed on
one of the panes, indicates the period of its erection by Sir Thos. Pakington, of Westwood
Park. The arms of the Pakingtons and their alliances with Washbourne, Baldwin, and
Kitson, are likewise emblazoned in this window. Both chancel and chapel are furnished
with plain piscinas in the usual position. The tower occupies the position and serves the
purpose of a south porch, as at Areley Kings, in this county. It consists of two stages:
on the south side of the lower one is a plain continuous archway, above which is a small
unfoliated square-headed window. The upper stage has in each face a two-light pointed
belfry window; and is capped by a projecting parapet, having battlements but no pinnacles.
Rising just above the parapet is a gabled roof, open at both ends, within which hangs the
small bell or "ting-tang." On the west side is a circular stair turret with conical cap dying
against the tower a little below the parapet. The *sanctus* bell-cot on the east gable of the
nave is very small, and can boast neither of bell nor ornament.

This church had fallen into a very dilapidated and unseemly state, when, about four years
ago, it was determined to restore it in a thoroughly substantial and correct manner. The
work has been carried out under the superintendence of Mr. Perkins, of Worcester; the whole
of the expense being defrayed by the Rt. Hon. Sir John S. Pakington, Bart., G.C.B.

New oak roofs have been erected over the chancel and chapel, and the latter portion of
the building rendered more available for congregational purposes, by opening a new arch
between it and the nave. The roof of the nave, though quite plain, was too good to remove;
it has therefore been repaired, and boarded at the back of the rafters. The stonework in the
interior has been denuded of plaster and colour-wash, and the masonry pointed; though
from its irregularity it is thought by some that the stonework of the walls was never
intended to be exposed to view. Be that as it may, the effect is, I think, undoubtedly
superior to colour-wash, and as undoubtedly inferior to appropriate fresco paintings: these
can, however, be supplied at any time. The ritual arrragements comprise an oak altar-table
standing on a foot-pace, carved oak rails and chairs, and a prayer desk and longitudinal
seat on the south side of the chancel only. The pulpit is of stone, the panels being enriched
with delicately carved diapers. The old traceried bench-ends have been used up in the
chapel, which is fitted with oak seats; those in the nave are of deal. The reredos is formed
of rich encaustic tiles, with which the chancel floor is also paved. Excellent stained glass,
by Hardman, fills the east window and one on the south side of the chancel. The former
contains the Ascension, the latter (a memorial window) S.S. Peter and Paul.

A remarkable instance of the little regard paid to the memory of an ancient and
distinguished member of an old family, by comparatively modern representatives of the

same family, was brought to light by the discovery, during the recent repairs, that a monument to the Sir John Pakington who died in 1727, which stood against the north wall of the sanctuary, had been placed in front of, and so as entirely to conceal, the tomb of the Sir John who died in 1551. This latter—a richly panelled Third-pointed structure, had been much mutilated, in order to facilitate the erection of its intrusive successor ; but is to be restored to its original state, thereby adding another object of historical and æsthetical interest to the church. The later monument supports a reclining statue of Sir John Pakington, supposed to have been the original of Sir Roger de Coverley : it has been removed to the west end of the chapel. There is a marble tablet to the present baronet's first wife, the daughter of M. A. Slaney, Esq., of Shiffnal, Salop. She died on the 6th Jan., 1843. Here is also a monument, with long Latin inscription, to Dr. Hammond.

The beautiful churchyard cross was restored in 1849, from a design by Mr. P. C. Hardwick. Round the top of the shaft are statuettes of the four Evangelists, under canopies, their symbols being carved on the upper portion of the base. On the west side of the latter is the following inscription :—

+ Ꜩo the beloved memory of Augusta Anne, second wife of Sir John S. Pakington, Bart., this Cross was restored, a.d. 1849; She was daughter of George Murray, lord bishop of Rochester, and departed this life in the true faith of Christ, February 23, 1848; after the birth of her second child, and in the 31st year of her age. + Not my will but thine be done.

The original " court-house stood, as was usually the case, near to the church. The mound, forming the eastern boundary of the churchyard, is formed by the remains of the old mansion, and the gardens extended on terraces down to the brook. Several of these terraces were visible a few years since, but are now almost entirely obliterated by the railway. The house must have been rebuilt by Sir John Pakington when he purchased the Hampton property (towards the end of the reign of Henry VII.) ; as Leland says, in his " Itinerary"— " Pakington hath a veri goodly new house of brike, called Hampton Court, vi mile of from Wircestre, somewhat northward." The old oil painting of this house preserved at Westwood represents it to have consisted of a square block of building, with a turret in the centre and smaller ones at the angles ; gabled wings projecting from the centre and forming with it three sides of a quadrangle. The large mullioned windows on each side of the entrance probably lighted a spacious and lofty hall, with a gallery round communicating with the upper rooms. This appears to have been an arrangement common to several of the old Worcestershire mansions, as at Severn End, Madresfield Court, and Witley Court : the original plan having been preserved at the latter throughout the various and extensive alterations it has undergone during the last and present centuries. Judging from the old painting only, I should be inclined to assign a somewhat later date to Hampton Court than the period of Leland's " Itinerary ;" but these quaint old views of buildings are not to be depended upon for architectural detail, which, indeed, they seldom attempt to give, and the perspective is often rather perplexing. In the annexed drawing, for instance, the turrets represented behind the wings, doubtless occupied a corresponding position at the back with those in front of the centre building; and it is most likely that there were four instead of three gables to the sides of the wings—one over each of the large windows beneath The Court-house having been much injured during the Civil Wars, the Lodge and Banquetting-house, which had been erected at Westwood in Queen Elizabeth's time, was enlarged by the addition of four wings, and made the family residence.

[The substance of the above account of Hampton Lovett, illustrated by a south-west view of the church, together with a description of Westwood, and a notice of some of the eminent divines connected with the history of the parish, was contributed by the Author to the Associated Architectural Societies' Annual Volume of "Reports and Papers" for 1859.]

Old Bewdley Bridge.

IT is evident that there was no bridge at Bewdley in 1313, for in that year the Prior and Convent of St. Mary's at Worcester complained to the Bishop of the great expense they were put to from the influx of strangers who came to pass the river at Worcester bridge, the only one between Bridgnorth and Gloucester.[*] We have no record when the first bridge was built here, but Henry VII. is said to have given the stone for the erection of one; which statement is not improbable, as Bewdley was at that time a place of considerable importance; the palace of Tickenhill adjoining the town having been built for the King's eldest son, Prince Arthur, who was married by proxy in the palace chapel, A.D. 1400, to Catherine of Arragon.

Though Leland, in describing the town, makes no mention of a bridge, there can be little doubt that the structure represented upon the accompanying plate was standing in his time. It was constructed upon the usual plan of Mediæval bridges, the arches being pointed, of no great span, and springing from massive oblong hexagonal piers. The triangular spaces formed by the parapets following the outline of the piers afforded convenient recesses in which foot passengers on the narrow roadway could retreat out of the way of vehicles, &c. On the centre of the bridge was one of the four gateways of the ancient borough; one side forming a prison, and the other a toll-house. Gateway-towers were a general feature of the old bridges; being used for the purposes of defence, also for taking toll, or as prisons, &c. Sometimes the room over the gateway was a chapel for the convenience of pilgrims, as at the west gate of Canterbury. The chapel, however, was more often a distinct building, and frequently of considerable architectural beauty. For instance, the chapel of St. Thomas of Canterbury, on old London bridge, had a range of mullioned windows on each side, and a richly groined crypt twenty feet in height; beneath which the original designer of the bridge, Peter of Colechurch, was buried. The best and most perfect of these chapels remaining is that on Wakefield bridge, Yorkshire. At Bewdley, the chapel is traditionally stated to have stood at the foot of the bridge, and to have been dedicated to St. Anne. The old

* Thomas's Survey of Worcester Cathedral, p. 160.

Old Bewdley Bridge,

From a Water colour Drawing at Stanford Court.

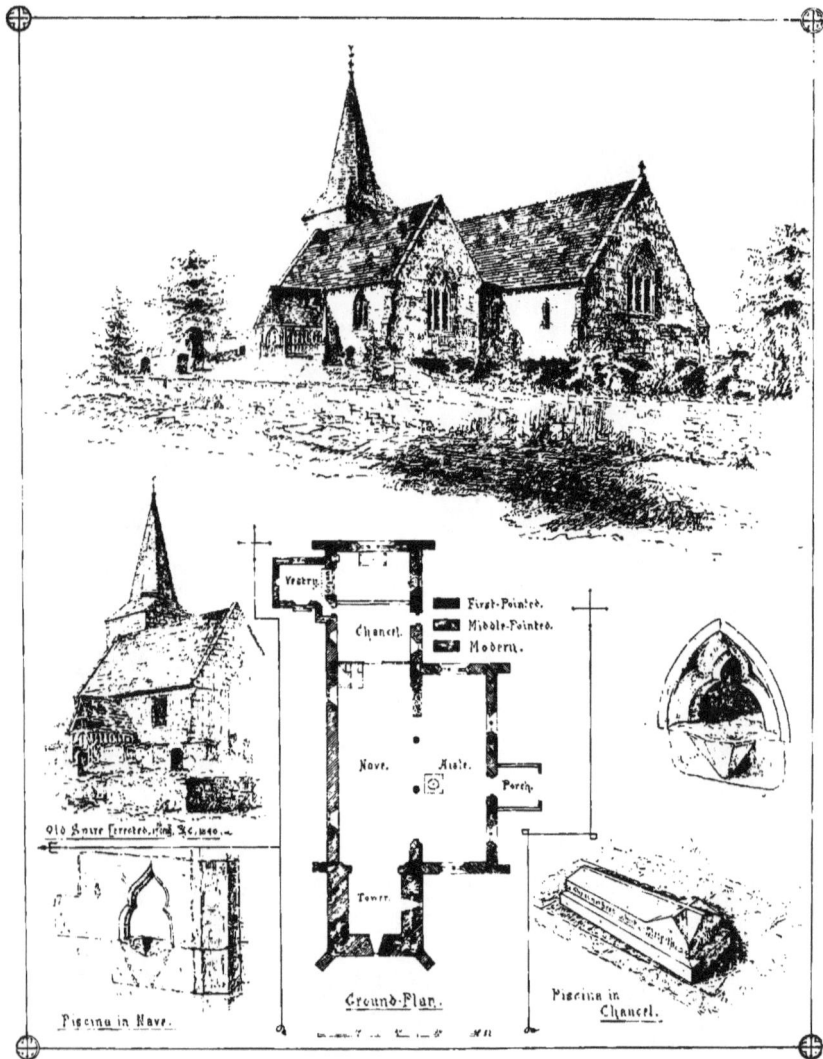

Legend in ground plan:
First-Pointed.
Middle-Pointed.
Modern.

Vestry.

Chancel.

Nave.   Aisle.

Porch.

Tower.

Old Spire Erected, Pind, &c., 1460.

Piscina in Nave.

Ground-Plan.

Piscina in
Chancel.

St. Kenelm's Church, Clifton upon Teme.

bridge* was taken down in 1797, when the present substantial structure was erected a little higher up the river, from the designs of Telford, the eminent engineer, then surveyor of the adjoining county of Salop.

Clifton-upon-Teme.

IF this parish cannot vie in architectural and antiquarian interest with some other localities, it stands preeminent for the salubrity of its air and the magnificent views its elevated position commands on every side, and which are bounded only by still loftier elevations. Amongst these may be mentioned the Wrekin and the Clee Hills, in Shropshire; the Radnor and Brecknockshire Mountains in Wales; the Cotswolds; the hills of Malvern, Bredon, Broadway, Clent, the Lickey, and the Ridgeway; the beauty and diversity of the landscape being further heightened by the minor hills which rise up within the rich intervening valleys of the Severn, the Avon, and the Teme; such as those of Abberley, Woodberrow, the Berrow, Ankerdine, Cruckberrow, the Old Hills, &c. On one side of the parish richly wooded dingles slope down towards the Teme, whilst on the other side the romantic Sapey brook sparkles through the most lovely dells it is possible to imagine. Clifton itself, as may be supposed, is visible at a great distance; the coronet of Scotch firs on the brow of the hill in Homme Castle park forming a distinguishing land-mark from all parts of the county. These trees are referred to by Southey in the following lines addressed to Mr. Cottle on his writing a poem entitled "*Malvern:*"—

> " Is Malvern then thy theme? it is a name
> That wakes in me the thoughts of other years,
> And other friends. Would I had been with thee
> When thou didst wind the heights, I could have loved
> To lead thee in the paths I once had trod,
> And pointing out the *dark and far-off fire*
> On *Clifton's, lofty summit*, or the spire that mark'd
> That pleasant town, that I must never more
> Without some heavy thoughts bethink me of.
> I could have lov'd to live the past again,
> Yet, were I ever more to tread those heights,
> Sure it should be in solitude; for since
> I travell'd there, and hath'd my throbbing brow
> With the drifted snows of the unsunn'd mountain cliff,
> Time hath much chang'd me, and that dearest friend†
> Who shar'd my wanderings, to a better world
> Hath past."

In the Conqueror's time Clifton belonged to Robert Fitz-Richard, of Richard's Castle. It afterwards came by marriage into the possession of Robert de Mortimer and William de Shuteville; and in the time of Henry IV. was conveyed to the Cliftons, Shuteville and Mortimer being still lords paramount. After being held by the Wyshams, of Woodmanton,

* Old Bedford Bridge was strikingly like the one at Bewdley, having a timber gateway in the centre, on one side of which was likewise a prison, where, according to some authorities, John Bunyan was confined. A view of it is given in the late Mr. Jabez Allies's "Antiquities and Folk-lore of Worcestershire."

† Mr. Edmund Seward, a young man of great promise, who lived in the adjoining parish of Lower Sapey, and died in 1795.

it came again to the Mortimers through Avice, wife of Sir John de Wysham, and thence descended to Richard, Duke of York, and King Edward IV. In the 6th of Edward VI., Henry Tracey conveyed it to William Jefferies, in which family it remained till the early part of the last century, when the manors of Clifton and Nether-Holme came into the possession of the Winningtons by the marriage of the third son of Sir Francis Winnington with the niece of Henry Jefferies, who died without issue in 1709.

Clifton was constituted a borough, 50th of Edward III., and was privileged with fairs, a weekly market on Tuesday, &c. The fairs have recently been revived, and are held at Easter and Michaelmas.

The church was appropriated to the nuns of Lymbroke, in Herefordshire, A.D. 1286. The portion reserved for the Vicar consisted of the alterage, certain sums from the churches of Stanford and Shelsley, the chapels of Sapey Pitchard and Edvin Loach, land in Clifton, and the house in which he lived, unless the nuns provided another. At the suppression of this monastery the advowson fell into the hands of John Callowhill, who disposed of it in the reign of Queen Mary to W. Jefferies, from whom it descended with the manor to Sir T. E. Winnington, Bart., the present lord of the manor and patron of the living.

This parish, though in the county of Worcester, is in the archdeaconry of Salop and diocese of Hereford.

The Church is one of the seven in England dedicated to St. Kenelm, the infant heir to the throne of Mercia, who was murdered on the Clent Hills, A.D. 819.

Its arrangement and styles are shown upon the accompanying ground plan. It differs from most of the churches in this neighbourhood in having no remains of Norman work. The tower must have been erected early in the succeeding style, being very plain and massive, and having the belfry stage pierced by narrow square-headed lights, except on the eastern side, where they are pointed. Opening into the nave is a wide and low continuous chamfered arch, constructed of *travertine*, a material of frequent occurrence in the old churches round here. Above the arch, immediately under the nave roof, is a triangular-headed opening. The arcade between the nave and aisle is quite plain, the arches resting upon octagonal piers, with a hood-moulding on the side next the aisle only. This aisle is supposed to have been erected by one of the Wyshams, of Woodmanton, his cross-legged effigy under the easternmost arch occupying the usual position of a founder's tomb. The eastern bay was originally screened off to form a chantry chapel. The piscina formerly in the south wall, has been removed to the north side of the sanctuary, where, with the addition of a stone shelf, it forms a credence. The font is hexagonal, diminishing in size from the top downwards, and placed upon an octagonal shaft, which in its turn becomes square. On the north side of the chancel was a low recessed and moulded arch, which the last Mr. Jefferies, in a MS. account of the parish, now at Stanford Court, says he " opened and under layd ye covering stone : 'twas rould down to ye bottome, and in it lyes a skeleton entire, who it seems had dispossest his p' decessor, for by his head there was thrown in a large skull not then decayed, ye bones ly a little moyst, wch keepe it from

The Church from yᵉ S-west.

Homme Castle.

Clifton upon Teme.

corruption." The arch was removed during the late alterations, and raised so as to form an opening between the sanctuary and the vestry for the organ to stand under, a method of utilizing an ancient tomb not by any means to be commended.

Nearly all the windows are modern. The old east window was almost the only Third-pointed work in the church; it contained considerable remains of ancient stained glass, which was unfortunately lost when the present Middle-pointed window was inserted in the rebuilt termination of the chancel, about 1843. The roofs are constructed on the common plan of collar-pieces and trussed rafters, which have always a good effect.

A partial, but not very satisfactory renovation of this church was effected about 1843, under the superintendence of the late Mr. Eginton, when new windows were inserted in the chancel and aisle, and the pews lowered. Since then a thorough restoration of the fabric has been carried out, chiefly during the incumbency of the Rev. G. Prothero, and from the designs of Mr. Cranston. An exceedingly handsome oak porch, a new vestry, and shingled spire, have been erected, the roofs and tower-arch opened, the gallery removed, massive deal seats substituted for pews, and a stone pulpit and oak prayer desk provided. The spire is fifty feet in height above the tower (which is forty feet high), being twenty feet lower than the original spire blown down in the 17th century, but considerably loftier than its immediate predecessor.

On the south side of the chancel are two painted windows, by Rogers; one representing the Raising of Lazarus, being to the memory of Lieut. R. W. Money Kyrle, who died in India, A.D. 1847; the other, Christ Blessing Little Children, is a memorial of the infant daughter of the Rev. G. Prothero, as is also the little coped tomb below the piscina. The three-light east window of the aisle has just been filled with rich stained glass, by Preedy, in memory of the late Martin Coucher, of Woodmanton, Esq., and two of his sons. The subjects represented are—the Baptism and the Temptation of our Lord, and Christ in the midst of the Doctors. The quatrefoils in the head of the window contain the arms of Wysham, Warren, and Poynings, in old glass. The church likewise contains several tablets to members of the Jefferies, Ingram, and other families; they possess no artistic merit; but over the vestry door is an interesting brass, erected by Sir T. E. Winnington, Bart., and bearing the following inscription :—

"Joyce Jefferies* of Hom Castle, who died in April, 1648, lies buried in this chancel.
Hom Castle gave her birth, Clifton a grave.
The simple records of her life attest
Her faith, her hope, her charity. From her home
At Hereford she fled; while civil war
Her lands sequestered and her dwellings razed;
And here she found repose—yet not a stone
For farewell line to mark her resting place,

* This worthy lady was great aunt to the last Mr. Jefferies, and resided for some years at Hereford, where she had several houses, which being destroyed in the civil wars she retired to her friend Mr. Geers's, at Garnons, and ultimately returned to the place of her birth. Her autograph Account-book "begininge at St. Mary Day, 1638," and extending over a period of nine years, is preserved at Stanford Court. It contains a very interesting record of the personal expenses, &c., of a lady of the upper classes in those stirring times; and formed the subject of two papers, read before the Society of Antiquaries in 1856, by the Rev. J. Webb, of Tretire, and which have been published in the *Archæologia.*

𝔒𝔯 𝔱𝔢𝔩𝔩 𝔱𝔥𝔢 𝔰𝔱𝔬𝔯𝔶 𝔬𝔣 𝔥𝔢𝔯 𝔠𝔥𝔢𝔮𝔲𝔢𝔯𝔢𝔡 𝔡𝔞𝔶𝔰.
𝔒𝔫𝔢 𝔴𝔥𝔬, 𝔞 𝔨𝔦𝔫𝔰𝔪𝔞𝔫, 𝔣𝔢𝔩𝔱 𝔰𝔲𝔠𝔥 𝔥𝔬𝔫𝔬𝔲𝔯 𝔡𝔲𝔢,
𝔓𝔞𝔶𝔰 𝔱𝔥𝔦𝔰 𝔩𝔞𝔱𝔢 𝔱𝔯𝔦𝔟𝔲𝔱𝔢, 𝔞𝔫𝔡 𝔦𝔫𝔰𝔠𝔯𝔦𝔟𝔢𝔰 𝔥𝔢𝔯 𝔱𝔬𝔪𝔟.

𝔄.𝔇. 1857."

There is a good plain double lich-gate over the entrance to the churchyard. The base and a portion of the shaft of the churchyard cross also remains.

𝔇𝔞𝔪𝔪𝔢, 𝔥𝔬𝔪𝔢, 𝔬𝔯 𝔇𝔞𝔪𝔪𝔢 𝔠𝔞𝔰𝔱𝔩𝔢, the ancient seat of the family of Jefferies, occupies a slightly elevated position in the valley of the Teme. It was injured by fire about 1582, and subsequently suffered greatly during the civil wars; some cannon balls of large size being preserved as memorials of the siege it then sustained. The only portion of the old *castle* remaining is a part of the well. The present house is a large half-timbered structure of the time of Charles II.; the dates 1677 and 1680, with the Jefferies arms—sable, a lion rampant between three scaling ladders, or—being on the hopper-heads of the rain-water pipes. There is a massive oak staircase, and the book-shelves of the old library in the roof still remain. Many of the MSS., &c., formerly preserved here, passed with the rest of the property to the Winningtons, and are now at Stanford Court.

The old terraces are perfect, but the exterior of the house lost much of its ancient character when it was coated with cement and other alterations made some five and twenty years ago. In the accompanying view, one gable is shown in its original state.

𝔚𝔬𝔬𝔡𝔪𝔞𝔫𝔱𝔬𝔫 is the most ancient, and was formerly, no doubt, the most important residence in the parish. In the 6th of Edward III., A.D. 1333, a license was granted to John de Wysham to crenellate (or fortify with battlements) his "manor of Wodemanton;"[*] and the existing remains of the old house appear to be of that date. The 𝔥𝔞𝔩𝔩 is tolerably perfect, and forms an interesting half-timbered example of the period. It has an open roof with collar-pieces and curved rafters, a moulded cornice at the sides, and a massive tie-beam in the centre. The arched braces beneath the latter are wanting; the south side and east end have been rebuilt with brick, and a floor introduced, so as to divide it into two stories, the lower one being used as a kitchen. The small portion of the roof westward of the Hall is of the same date, but of plainer construction. It is probable that the building extended farther eastward, as the roof timbers at this end are visible from the outside. Built into an out-house is the head of a three-light 𝔴𝔬𝔬𝔡𝔢𝔫 𝔴𝔦𝔫𝔡𝔬𝔴 belonging to the hall or some other part of the old house. The present house was built about 35 years ago: it is a plain brick structure of no architectural pretensions, occupying a portion of the site of the older dwelling, and projecting southward from the west end of the ancient building above described. At the inner north-west angle of the moat,—which was partially filled up at the time the house was rebuilt,—is what appears to be the foundation of a circular stone tower—a relic, perhaps, of the fortifications John de Wysham was licensed to erect.

The Wyshams were a family of importance in these parts during the 13th and 14th centuries, and had possessions at Churchill and other places in the county. At the death of the above-named John, the elder branch became extinct, but the younger descendants

* Parker's "Domestic Architecture in England," part iii., p. 410.

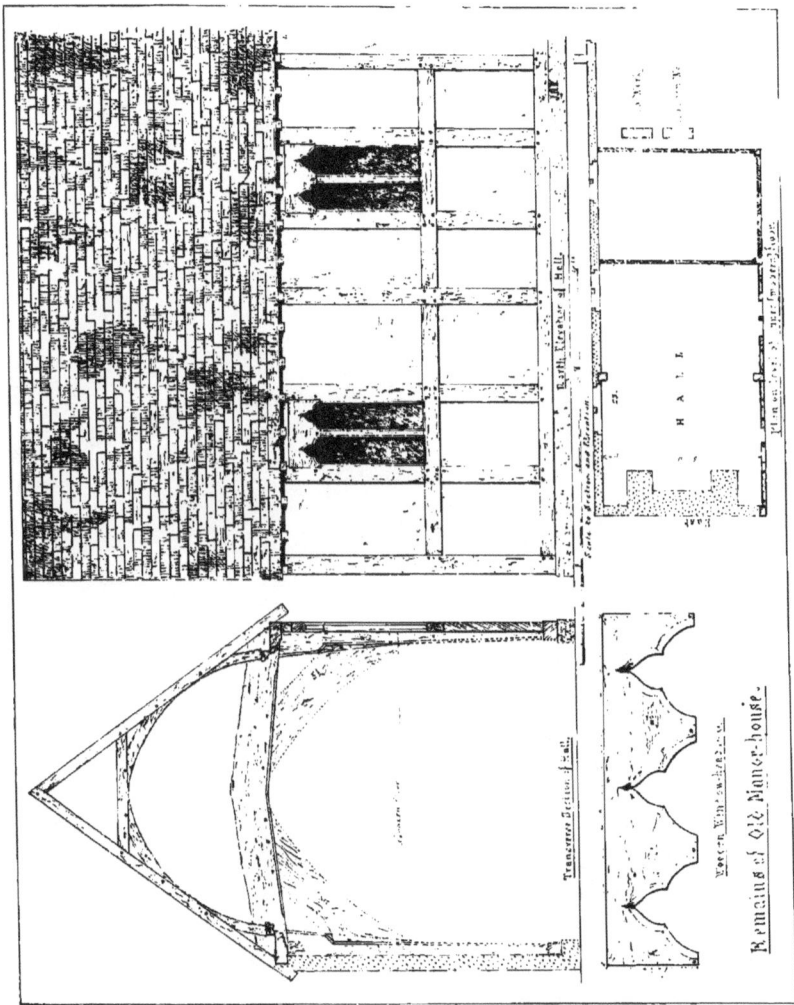

Remains of Old Manor-house.

Transverse Section of Hall.

Western Entrance Door.

East Window of Hall.

HALL

Plan of the Ground Floor.

Woodmanton, Clifton upon Teme.

Old Church - Knightwick.

New Church of S. Mary.

Porch - Old Church of S. Andrew - Dodenham.

Porch - Knightwick old Church.

Knightwick and Dodenham.

continued to reside in the adjoining parish of Tedstone Delamere some time longer. The Jefferies family are supposed to have intermarried with the Wyshams, their arms impaling Wysham being formerly in a window at Homme Castle.

Woodmanton was sold in 1569 by John Callowhill, of Tedstone Delamere, to John Coucher, of Worcester, and has remained in the same family ever since, it being now the property of Martin S. Coucher, Esq., M.D., of Weymouth.

There is no record as to how or when this estate became separated from the manor of Clifton, with which it was formerly held, but to which it is now subordinate, paying chief-rent to the lord of that manor.

The Lion Inn near the church is thought to have formed a part of the old court-house. Mr. Jefferies, in the MS. before quoted, says—"The manner-place was ye hous now known by ye name of ye Red Lyon, an in which ye Ramseys have held it at will for three generations. Before my father built ye midle part of it, there was a great hall open to ye top, with a fire-place in ye midle, and a lantern on top, collegiate fashion, and in pt of ye old hous yet standing is a chamber called ye Court Chamber, for yt ye courts I pr'sume were then held there, and neer adjoining is a piece of land, which hitherto retaines ye name of ye Hall Orchard." There is nothing of architectural interest connected with the house at the present time.

There are several other houses in the parish dating from about the middle of the 17th century; though much modernized, as *The Noke*, *The Hope*, and *Salford*. At the latter is a fine stack of chimneys and a noble kitchen.

Knightwick and Dodenham.

THE Prior of Great Malvern, to which monastery Knightwick anciently belonged, surrendered the manor to Bishop Godfrey Gifford and his successors to hold the same, paying a pound of cummin; the deed being dated the Saturday next after the feast of All Saints, in the 11th year of Edward I., and confirmed by the King November 7th the same year at Acton Burnel. In the 6th year of Edward III., the Bishop granted the manor to William de Masyngton and Agnes his wife, at the rent of five marks yearly; and in 1460, John, Bishop of Worcester let to Thomas Rumpney of Lullesley, Isabel his wife, and William their son, the site of his manor of Knightwick, with houses, lands, rents of tenements, &c., at the yearly rent of £8. The family of Alderford had lands in this parish, which in the reign of Elizabeth passed to John Washborne, and afterwards belonged to John Clent.

The manor of Dodenham, a chapelry in this parish, was granted to the priory of Worcester previously to the year 1179; and soon afterwards Simon de Manus, for the health of his soul, and the souls of his wife and ancestors, gave to the church of Worcester the advowson of Dodenham and Knightwick—Walter de Ancredham, and many other possessors of property here, were also benefactors to the priory of Worcester: and several exchanges of land took place between the Prior and Adam lord of Ancredham, a manor in this chapelry.

We learn the quantity of agricultural stock and implements upon the manors of Dodenham and Ancredham in the time of Richard II. from a lease of those manors granted by the Prior and convent to Richard Cowarne and John Damalis, citizens of Worcester—viz., " 8 oxen, value 8 marks, ten cows, value 100 shillings, one long wain ironed, value 13 shillings, one gander, four geese, one cock, six hens, one cart, one plough, one harrow, one horse, with three loads of good hay." The lessees were to pay " at the four usual terms of the year the sum of eight pounds, binding themselves and their heirs and executors in a bond of ten pounds, to leave the same stock thereon at the end of the term."

F. E. Williams, Esq., of Malvern Hall, Warwickshire, and J. Freeman, Esq., of Gaines, are now the principal landed proprietors in Knightwick and Dodenham.

The old Churches at both these places were of simple and rude construction; each consisting of chancel, nave, south porch, and the wooden bell-turret which is so common in this neighbourhood. The open timber porches formed the best external feature; the one at Knightwick being of early character; that at Dodenham Elizabethan or Jacobean. There were one or two Norman windows in this latter chapel, and the roof was really an *open* one, never having been ceiled, even between the rafters.

The three-light east window at Knightwick is Middle-pointed, the centre light being carried up to the top of the arch, a description of window which very frequently occurs in this county and in Herefordshire. On the floor of the nave is a stone to the memory of Grace Lane, niece to the Mistress Jane Lane who assisted Charles II. in his escape: she died in 1721, aged 80. This church is now only used at funerals, the surrounding churchyard continuing to serve as the parochial burial ground; and the chapel at Dodenham has been entirely removed.

In place of the above dilapidated old structures the new Church of St. Mary has been erected in a most picturesque spot at the foot of Ankerdine Hill. It was designed by Mr. Perkins, of Worcester, and is a pleasing example of a small country church, consisting of chancel, vestry, nave, north porch, and octagonal bell-turret rising from a central buttress at the west end. The chancel is spacious, and, with the addition of some stained glass and decorative colour, the interior would be very effective; the *plastered* chancel arch being the only important blemish.

At the suppression of the Cathedral monastery the patronage passed to the Dean and Chapter.

The scenery of this neighbourhood is very beautiful, and the view from Ankerdine Hill is scarcely inferior to the prospect commanded by the more important hills of Malvern and Bredon.

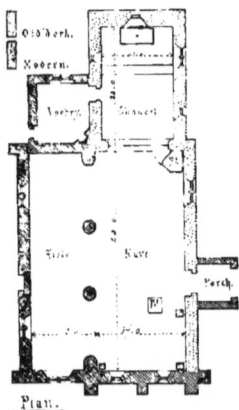

Plan.

Lectern.

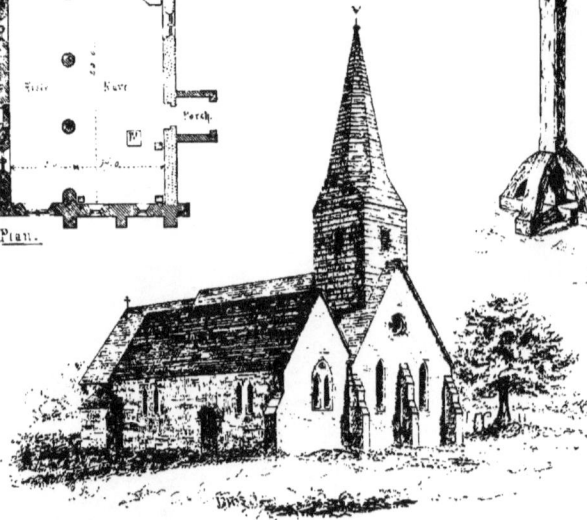

North-west View.
As Enlarged - 1861.

Font.

Window, & steps to Rood-loft
formerly in Nave.

White Ladies Aston Church.

White Ladies' Aston.

THIS parish was formerly called *Eston Episcopi*, being situated eastward of the Cathedral monastery, and forming an appendage of the Bishop's manor of Northwick.

In King John's reign, Rafe de Wylyton, with the consent of his wife Olympia, and his heirs, granted the manor and patronage "to God, St. Mary the Virgin, the mother church of Worcester, and Silvester, Bishop of Worcester." Other grants were made to the succeeding Bishops, William de Bloys and Walter de Cantelupe. The latter gave fifty-one acres of land in Eston, purchased of Robert de Bracey, to the Nuns or "White Ladies" of Whiston, to whom Bishop Godfrey Gifford made a further grant of the manor and patronage, reserving to himself a third part of the lands. Since this time the parish has borne the name of White Ladies' Aston.

After the Dissolution the manor and patronage were granted by the King to Richard Andrews and John Howe. They were subsequently held by the families of Hill, Gowre, and Andrews, being at length purchased by Mr. Rowland Berkeley, of Spetchley, in which family the manor and advowson still remain.

Sir Hugh de Eston had an estate here in the thirteenth century, which afterwards belonged to a Mr. Symonds, a great favourite of Oliver Cromwell, who is said to have made his head quarters at Mr. Symonds's house before the battle of Worcester.

A descendant of the above Mr. Symonds was executed in 1708 for helping to commit a dreadful murder, when the estate fell to the Bishop of the diocese, who, being unwilling to enjoy the fruits of such a crime, devoted it to the endowment of the school at Worcester known as "Bishop Lloyd's School."

The Church in its original state was a very simple structure, consisting of chancel and nave of the Norman period, with western bell-turret and a modern brick porch. Several of the old Norman windows remain, including a single-light at the east end; and in the splay of the one on the north side of the nave were the remains of the steps which led to the rood-loft. The north and south doorways (the former removed to the new aisle) are of the same early style, and quite plain. A Middle-pointed square-headed window has been inserted in the south wall of the nave, and a Third-pointed one on the same side of the chancel. The lofty spirelet rests upon massive wooden framework in the interior of the church, at the west end.

The general condition of the building being unsatisfactory, and the accommodation insufficient, it was determined to add a north aisle to the nave and re-arrange the whole of the interior. Plans for these alterations were prepared by Mr. W. J. Hopkins, of Worcester; and the works having been successfully carried out, the church was reopened in May, 1861. The new aisle is in the Early-pointed style, and is divided from the nave by three arches composed of light and dark tinted stone in alternate courses, and resting upon piers with moulded caps and bases. Eastward of the aisle is a vestry. The west end of the nave has

D

been rebuilt; two lancets, divided by a buttress with a quatrefoil above, being inserted therein instead of the wooden domestic windows which previously existed in the gable. The chancel fittings, lectern, and pulpit, are of oak; the nave seats of deal, and very commodious. The altar rail is supported by foliated wrought-iron standards, and the floor is paved with red and blue tiles. The opening of the roofs, the restoration of the old walls, and the erection of a new porch, were obliged to be deferred for want of funds; for it was only by the most untiring exertions that the vicar, the Rev. H. M. Sherwood, was enabled to raise a sufficient sum to defray the cost of the much-needed alterations just described, the parishioners consisting entirely of tenant-farmers and labourers.

Cofton Hackett.

URSO D'ABITOT and his heirs, the Beauchamps, were originally lords of Cofton; the families of Cofton and Leycester holding lands under them. The Coftons becoming extinct in the time of Edward IV. were succeeded by the Hodyngtons, the Russels, and the Winters. Matilda Hacket, wife of Robert de Leycester, held lands here 20th of Edward III.; hence its additional name. Cofton Hacket afterwards came to the Dineleys, and thence to Mr. Edward Skinner, a rich clothier of Ledbury, whose granddaughter married Thomas Jolliffe; and his grandson, Thomas Jolliffe, dying in 1758, left the property to his niece, Rebecca Lowe, for life; and upon her death to his nephew, Michael Biddulph, of Ledbury; it now belongs to the Baroness Windsor, of Hewell Grange.

The college of Westbury, near Bristol, possessed lands at Groveley in this chapelry. Upon the suppression of the house it was granted to Sir Ralph Sadler, and afterwards passed to the Litteltons, of Pillaton, in the county of Stafford.

Cofton is a chapelry to Northfield; a large parish extending hence to Birmingham. The chapel of S. Michael stands close to the Birmingham and Bristol railway, and is a small but interesting structure; the ground plan consisting of chancel, nave, and south porch. The chancel is Middle-pointed; the walls of the nave also appear to belong to the same style, though raised, and square-headed windows inserted, during the Third-pointed period. Of the latter style is the rather clumsy double bell-gable at the west end, below which is a massive central buttress, effectively relieving the otherwise perfectly plain and unbroken wall-surface.

On the north side of the sanctuary is an interesting incised alabaster slab, representing William Leycester and his two wives. Above the figures are three shields bearing the arms of *Leycester*, *Cofton*, *Blundell*, *Heird*, and *Worley*; below are two children, with this inscription :—" Non intres in judicium cum animabus filiorum tuorum ;" and round the edge of the slab is the following inscription, as given by Nash :—" Hic jacent corpora Wilhelm Leycester, domini de Cofton Haket, et Elianorœ et Annœ uorum suarum ; qui

St Michael's Ch: Cofton-Hackett.

Worcestershire.

Font.

Alebaster inlaid slab.

Barnt-Green House: Worcestershire.

Grammar School: Kingsnorton.

quidam Wilhelmus obiit die . . . . 1508. Elianora fuit filia Edmundi Worley arm. et obiit 7 die mensis Januarii, An. Dom. 1514. Quarum animabus propitietur Deus. Amen." The names of Lyttelton, Skinner, Dineley, Jolliffe, and others, also appear on memorials here. I have rarely met with a more absurdly fulsome epitaph than the following to Mr. Thomas Jolliffe, who died in the last century :—"Integrity and Benevolence were so conspicuously combined in his character, that it is difficult to determine whether the public spirit of the patriot, or the social virtues of the man, rendered him most valuable. He loved his friends much, his country more ; in the love of both he was equally disinterested and inflexible. Humanity dictated and good sense directed his unbounded charity. He possessed an uncommon knowledge of the world, *but was free from its corruptions* (?) ; his peculiar sagacity taught him the first, his christian principles preserved him from the latter. His agreeable conversation, his vivacity unalloyed by malignity, contributed to soften that reverence which was raised by his nobler qualities into the gentleness of sincere affection. The patience with which he expected, and the resignation with which he sustained, the hour of death, can only be paralleled by the vigilance and assiduity of her who closed his dying eyes. The gratitude and filial duty, with which she always regarded the paternal love of her deceased Uncle, have erected this monument to those virtues which she must for ever remember and lament."

The validity of the will by which this paragon of perfection left the whole of his property to " her who closed his dying eyes" was contested by the male heirs on the ground of the testator's insanity. Judgment was, however, given in favour of the lady.

There is a good modern brass (a cross) to the late John Merry, Esq., of Groveley ; the painted east window is a memorial to Mrs. Merry.

This little church has recently undergone a thorough restoration. The plaster and whitewash have been removed from the roofs and walls, a chancel arch erected, open deal seats provided for the nave, and a new floor and heating apparatus laid down. The well executed chancel seats, lectern, and pulpit, of carved oak, and the handsome new stone font— a special gift—were designed by Mr. Dudley Male, of London, who superintended the restoration of the chancel generally, on behalf of the Rector ; the works in the nave having been carried out, on behalf of the Baroness Windsor, from drawings furnished by Mr. H. Day, of Worcester. The half-timbered porch has been most unaccountably covered with cement, *jointed in imitation of stone !*

Cofton Hall is situated a little to the south of the church. The principal part of the house was erected in the last century, but the kitchen is formed out of a portion of the old hall of the original mansion, and has a fine Third-pointed roof in a good state of preservation.

Near to Cofton, but in the parish of Alvechurch, is Farnt Green House, a picturesque half-timbered structure, whose numerous gables and nicely laid-out grounds are seen to great advantage from the railway, which is here carried on a high embankment.

The old house is the property of the Baroness Windsor, and the residence of her Ladyship's agent, Mr. Tomson.

Free School, Kingsnorton.

This school is supposed to have been founded by Edward VI. about the same time as the far more important one at Birmingham. It is said that the Kingsnorton men chose a money endowment, and those of Birmingham preferred land; the consequence being that the former school receives only some £15 a year, the amount of the original endowment, while the latter establishment has an annual income of £9,000 or £10,000, owing to the greatly increased value of land in that populous neighbourhood.

The School-house stands on the north side of the churchyard, and is a late Pointed structure; though the three-light traceried wooden window in the principal gable appears to belong to the Middle-pointed style: it may possibly have been brought from some other building, but early forms were often imitated in the wood-work of a much later date.

Thomas Hall, a rigid Puritan writer and divine, is stated to have been master of the school at Kingsnorton, and afterwards "preacher of the word" at the time when the lawfully ordained parish priests were almost everywhere dispossessed of their churches "by the authority of Parliament." He died in 1665, and bequeathed to the school and parish a library of between six and seven hundred volumes—chiefly of the controversial divinity of that period—which still remain in the upper room of the old school-house.

Beauchamp Lodge and Roadway-Hill Cottage, Highnam Court, Gloucestershire.

WE cannot but regret the gradual disappearance of the picturesque old timbered houses, which harmonize so well with the scenery of this well-wooded country, and whose places are generally supplied by buildings quite out of keeping with the surrounding natural objects, and forming anything but pleasing objects in the landscape.

Now that brick and stone are so accessible, and wood is comparatively scarce, it is not likely that the old method of building will again become general. Still it might be adopted with propriety and advantage much oftener than it is; though the modern examples we sometimes see are not calculated to induce us to think favourably of the applicability of the style to the requirements of the present day, it being too often fantastic and toy-like.

Some remarkably good examples of small half-timbered houses have, however, been erected by T. Gambier Parry, Esq., on his estate at Highnam. The annexed drawings represent two of them, built in 1859, from the designs of Messrs. Hugall and Male, of London.

Beauchamp-Lodge. Highnam Court: Gloucester.

Highnam Court : Glouc. Roadway-Hill Cottage

+ S-East View 1863.

[From "Mau's History of Evesham" 1824]

North Doorway

S. Egwin's Church, Norton, near Evesham.

www.ingramcontent.com/pod-product-compliance
Lightning Source LLC
Chambersburg PA
CBHW021635270326
41931CB00008B/1039